# HOW TO STOP DATING DICKHEADS

\*\*\*

DISCLAIMER

This book is NOT a therapeutic treatment or substitute for therapy

No, you don't have a dickhead magnet on your head!

You don't!!

And no, you aren't destined to attract dickheads forever.

This guide is going to break that cycle for you, once and for all!

Right you fabulous human, step away from the wine and chocolate, get your head out of the ice-cream tub, off the online dating apps, stop stalking your ex's social media and let's take some useful action.

You're too good, and your life is too precious, to be stuck in a cycle of dating dickheads - this shit changes now, OK?

Let's go!

# I know my stuff about dickheads...

Once upon a time I was training to become a counsellor. Every week in our practice counselling sessions I would rant and rave about my dickhead ex-husband, or the latest new dickhead I'd accumulated while simultaneously trying to rebuild my life after the fall-out of the marriage to the dickhead.
I should probably point out that there had also been numerous dickheads before the marriage - I'd got stuck in a terrible dickhead cycle.

I remember my very funny, and very lovely counselling tutor saying, *'It's honestly like they've all been given copies of the dickhead manual!'* because the similarities between her dickhead ex husband and mine were startling.

And over the years, as I've listened to more and more stories told to me by heartbroken women about the carnage left behind by their dickhead ex partners it definitely becomes more and more apparent that somewhere out there really is a 'dickhead manual' and these jokers that we've ended up in relationships with have memorised it line by line.

So, in this age of awakening women, it's time we had a manual of our own. A manual to stop the cycle of dating dickhead after dickhead.

I've written you the manual I wish I'd had 10 years ago.

Let my mess and my dickhead disasters become your survival guide.

Learn from me and never get stuck with another dickhead ever again.

Beware though, this isn't a fluffy nicey nicey airy fairy read.

I see things in a very straightforward fashion and I tell it as I see it.

Some of what I tell you in this guide will sting like a bitch, because it will cause you to look at yourself.

This is a guide, but it's also a workbook, so that means there's work to be done.

The dickhead cycle doesn't stop itself as if by magic.

If you've already identified that you're stuck in a cycle of dickheads, I can't emphasise this enough - DO THE WORK!!

Your future self, in a fabulously happy relationship will thank you for it.

Let's start with what to do, and what you need
to know, after a recent break up

Allow yourself to have feelings

(It's perfectly OK to feel shite)

I've spent hundreds and hundreds of hours in counselling rooms with clients. I know a thing or two about the effect of suppressing emotion.

Emotion is energy, and the main rule of energy is that it likes to MOVE.

*Energy hates to get stuck.*

So, right now, the best thing you can do for yourself is to *keep your emotional energy moving.*

How do you do that?

Cry. Scream. Shout. Rant. Rave.

Do whatever you need to do to keep that emotion moving safely.

Journal, talk to friends or a therapist, dance, walk, complete this guide.

Don't pretend your OK when you're not. Be real with yourself and if you feel like shit (which most people do after a break up) give yourself full permission to feel shit.

Something I've observed over the years is that *the quicker we acknowledge our unpleasant emotion, allow it to be, and stop trying to sprinkle positivity all over it, the quicker it moves by itself.*

Don't torture yourself playing
the self-blame game


(When someone shows you their true
colours - don't wait for them to show
you twice!)

Oh I know how painful this can be, and sadly this seems to happen particularly when you've been cheated on or monumentally dumped. The painful plummet down the rabbit hole of 'what did I do wrong?', 'if only I'd done this differently', 'if only I'd done that differently', it can be absolute torture. So know you're not alone in doing this - it's quite a natural thing to do.

I suggest writing it all down. All of those thoughts running through your head - all of them. Write them down. Don't try and ignore them, they'll only scream and shout for more attention. Give them the attention to shut them up.

Answer all of your own questions.

When you're in this self-blame place after a break up, your brain is frantically trying to make sense of what's happened, so let it do exactly that.

Give it answers.

Write down all the questions you're torturing yourself with, and answer them as best you can. Go there. What could you have done wrong? What could you have done differently?

Learn anything you need to learn.

But know this. If someone cheated, *it's never about you*.

It's *always* about them. Cheating is a choice. It's a decision someone makes to consciously hurt their partner. It's as simple as that.

I have no judgement around this. Life happens and people do what they do. But ultimately people are in control of their actions and always have a choice.

And also know this...

Absolutely beautiful, stunning, intelligent, funny, amazing women get cheated on. So you can quit the 'it was because I was fat, boring, stupid' kind of thoughts. Those things are your brain lying to you. Those things are shock and emotional pain and low self-esteem talking - they are NOT THE TRUTH.

When a partner makes a choice to cheat, it's never something that the other person did wrong - there's never anything they could've done differently.

The dickhead they'd chosen chose to hurt them.

End of story.

So take a deep breath and know that not all people are bad. All relationships don't and won't end in this way.

This too shall pass, and much better relationship experiences are waiting for you at the end of all of this.

You've got this, and because you're here, reading this and taking the time to focus on you, you're going to be OK.

Forgive YOURSELF

(The question should never be 'how do I forgive myself?
The real question to ask is 'why am I choosing to
continuously punish myself?')

If you can't forgive yourself for dating a dickhead (or in my case many) you're going to have a life of pain and suffering all of your own making, and you might as well just keep dating the dickheads if you want that kind of life.

Forgiveness is such a precious gift you can give yourself, and it really is as simple as making a choice.

Will you forgive yourself or not?

And, if the choice is (and I hope it is) to forgive - you have to keep making that choice over and over again until it's become habitual. Forgiveness is an ongoing practice.

Because here's the thing. You've already had a shit time. You ended up with a dickhead and you're absolutely not the first, and you definitely won't be the last to fall for the charms of a dickhead and to be left feeling like an absolute plum.

Falling for a dickhead doesn't make you a bad person.

Falling for a dickhead doesn't make you some sort of criminal.

Falling for a dickhead doesn't mean you should be punished.

So why kick yourself when you're already down? What will that achieve?

You're human.

And being human is hard.

Bloody hard.

There's reasons you fell for a dickhead.

You're identifying those now, and taking steps to stop yourself falling into the dickhead trap again.

In my book, that makes you a fucking legend.

So, straighten your crown, remind yourself that actually, you're frigging awesome and lets keep moving.

This whole dickhead cycle is soon to be a thing of the past.

You WILL feel better

(I know, I know, you don't believe me yet)

When the relationship first comes to an end it sets the rollercoaster of unpleasant emotion off at full speed. It doesn't matter if you ended it, or the dickhead ended it - it ended and it's going to stir up emotion.

I can't emphasise this next thing enough, so I'm saying it again;

DO NOT TRY AND IGNORE THE EMOTION!!!!!!!!!!!!!!!!!!!!!!!!!!!!!!!!

Emotion is NOT the enemy.

Emotion is energy and it needs to move - let it move.

The end of a relationship tends to spark off these emotions in particular;

Anger

Sadness

Regret

Anxiety

It's very similar to the grief we experience when someone dies.

You can end up feeling like an absolute basket case but you're not. *You're processing a loss.* Allow yourself full permission to feel that loss.

When emotions are acknowledged and allowed to run their course, they do exactly that - they run their course.

These painful and unpleasant feelings that you're experiencing WILL PASS.

Help yourself as much as you possible can to ride out these emotions.

Put a date in your diary - one month from now.

Rate how you feel today out of ten - ten is amazing - zero is absolutely shite.

Now, write the number you want to feel in one month time.

And answer these two questions;

What 3 things could I STOP doing now to help improve how I feel over the next month;

- 
- 
- 

And...

What 3 things can I START doing now to help improve how I feel over the next month

- 
- 
- 

Hopefully one of the things you put on your things to start was completing reading this guide because this is really going to help you get your head and heart back in a good place.

*Your energy and focus needs to be on you now.*

Commit to making your happiness and your health a priority.

The one relationship you can 100% guarantee that you're going to be in for the rest of your life is the one you have with yourself. It's the most important and precious relationship you'll ever have and it's the one, in my humble opinion, that always needs the most love and effort.

You'll be with you for the rest of your life, it's so much nicer, easier and happier when you get along.

Every other relationship that comes along after that, it simply an added bonus.

There really are more fish in the sea


(And the next one you catch won't be some slimy little
horror show - it'll be a fish worth actually catching)


- That's if you even want another fish! -

When you're at that awful point when a relationship has just come to an end, it's easy to think that you'll never find someone else.

That it's just going to be you and your ten thousand cats until the end of your miserable days, but that is utter bullshit.

And your first question needs to be this;

*Do you even want to catch another fish?*

Because here's the thing...

YOU DON'T ACTUALLY HAVE TO BE IN A RELATIONSHIP AT ALL.

Mind-blowing right?

Back in the day I believed I was unlovable and quite honestly a useless human if I wasn't in a relationship. It scared me more than anything to be alone. I was always so desperate for love and attention that I'd fling myself at anything that threw me a scrap of 'love'.

Which of course led to dickheads taking advantage.

So use this time to get clear on that first of all - *do you want a relationship, or do you just think you should have one, or need to have one?*

And get lovingly curious around your responses to those questions.

Because of course, if you do indeed want a relationship, then there are billions of people on this planet - the perfect one for you is out there.

*But you won't find the perfect one until you stop settling for the dickhead ones. It's that simple.*

You keep rejecting the ones that aren't good enough until you find the one that is.

Most of us miss out this step. We're so pleased to get *anything* that we daren't bin someone in case that was the best we were ever going to get.

If you have this mindset - change it! Because it's keeping you in the dickhead cycle.

*If you want to end the dickhead cycle you have to remember your courage.*

You have to remember that being alone is better than being with a dickhead.

And *you have to get OK with saying no to what isn't good enough.*

It's like buying a new car. If you have your heart set on a Range Rover Velar, and you have the money for a Range Rover Velar, but keep walking out of the car place with a Vauxhall Meriva because it was the first shiny looking one in the showroom then you're never going to have a Range Rover Velar.

Rose tinted glasses only look good on
Elton John


(And, to be fair, they're not really even a good look
on him)

Nobody else will tell you to do this bit of work, but it's crucial you do.

Your mind is going to play tricks on you now that you're out of a relationship with a dickhead.

It's going to tell you that they weren't that bad. They were lovely most of the time and most of the time is good enough, it'll say.

It's going to do this because your brain doesn't like the fact that you're in emotional pain right now and so it's looking for solutions to fix it.

Your brain can be a total legend and it can also be a total prick.

It's not it's fault, it's just how brains work.

Brains are one huge data storage system and *it's your job to filter out what's useful to listen to and what isn't.*

Your brain is going to try to tell you the rose tinted story about the dickhead so rather than ignoring that story and trying to suggest you just force yourself to hate them, I want you to *get clear on what the rose tinted version is.* You need to know this so that when your brain throws it at you during times of loneliness and boredom, you can see it for what it is - *a bullshit rose tinted story.*

Here's an example from one of my own past dickheads;

<u>*Rose-tinted story*</u>;

He bought me flowers and surprised me with lovely gifts. He told me how much he loved me. He'd hold me and kiss my forehead and those are the best kisses. He'd stand up for me. He made an effort with my friends and family. He wanted to be with me. He loved me.

<u>*Reality*</u>;

He spat in my face.
He called me names and threatened to kill me.
He stole from me.
He cheated on me. Many times.

Do you see the powerful effect of the rose tinted glasses?

Use the next two pages to get really clear about what your rose tinted story is and what the actual reality is.

Your words will always always be more powerful than the words of someone else.

My rose tinted story is....

The reality of my story is....

_____

_____

_____

_____

_____

_____

_____

_____

_____

_____

_____

_____

_____

_____

_____

_____

_____

_____

_____

*Now, take a highlighter pen, re-read your reality story and highlight the parts that were the very definition of dickhead.*

The parts where they treated you like shit.

Where they disrespected you.

Where they acted like a total nobhead.

Where they embarrassed you.

Where they were inconsiderate.

The stuff that if it had happened to your friend, daughter or sister you'd be in the car barefoot like a shot ready to kick their head in on their behalf!

You know the sort of stuff I mean - get it highlighted.

You cannot forget this stuff!

These things that you highlight are going to save you from dickheads like this again and become part of your own survival guide, so don't miss any - get them written down and highlighted.

When you're drowning, you don't stop to inspect the life jacket you've been thrown

(You just grab the bloody thing and hold on for dear life!)

Often, one of the reasons we fall for dickheads, and they slip under our dickhead radar. is because when they came along we were 'drowning'.

Potentially we met them when we were recently bereaved, or in financial difficulty, or a good old fashioned rebound from another relationship.

Basically when we were vulnerable for some reason.

The analogy I've always used with my clients is this one;

Look, if you're out at sea drowning (i.e. emotionally suffering in some way) and someone throws you a life jacket, you don't waste your time checking the stitching, making sure it's the right life jacket for you etc etc - you just grab the bloody thing and hang on for dear life.

And often that's what we do with relationships with dickheads. They came along at a time when we were struggling- they looked like a potential aid to that suffering so we grabbed hold of them.

That doesn't mean you have to walk around with a life jacket on your whole life. When you've steadied yourself and regained your strength, give yourself permission to let the lifejacket go if it's not serving you any more.

Anger is natural


(But you will NOT enjoy prison!)

Googling 'how much is a hitman?' is very natural when you've ended a relationship with a dickhead.

Being angry is natural.

It does NOT make you a bad person!

Let the anger move - just remember this;

STAY OUT OF PRISON!!!

Dickheads are not worth doing time for!!

So, rant to your friends, rip up photos, buy a dartboard or punchbag and let that anger move.

*Make a note of safe ways that you can release and vent your anger;*

- 
- 
- 
- 
- 
- 
- 
- 
-

## And here's the thing about anger...

Sitting in your living room, chewing yourself up with anger, is a path to self-destruction.

It is, in very simple terms, like drinking poison yourself and expecting it to magically then kill the person you're thinking about while you drink it.

*It's not going to have the slightest little effect on them!*

But it is going to 'kill' you.

It's going to raise your anxiety and ruin your peace.

You always have a choice., so choose your own peace every time.

When the angry thoughts about the dickhead come along - write them down and then burn them. Do that as many times as you need to to keep clearing that crappy energy from your life.

You deserve more than a life filled with poison.

You really are better off without them


(Only loneliness, boredom and low self-esteem will make
you think otherwise)

Loneliness, boredom and low self-esteem are potentially going to attack you and I want you to be ready for that.

When your dickhead comes crawling back (because 9 times out of 10 they do) you need to be ready - really ready.

Because just like the crisps and biscuits in the cupboard tell you that it won't hurt to just have one or two, you know full well you won't stop at one or two, you'll have the whole packet and then you'll kick yourself.

The same will happen with the dickhead. He'll send you some needy message one night, with a half-arsed apology and the promise of him 'changing'. You'll be bored, lonely and feel worried that you'll never find anyone else and before you know it you've slept with the dickhead, he's ghosting you again and you see him draped around someone else on his social media and you're crying into your nachos.

*You need to have a ready made set of 'weapons' for the inevitable boredom, loneliness and the feeble crawling back of the dickhead.*

#I - Block and delete the dickhead.

Facebook, Instagram, WhatsApp, whatever way he can contact you - *block him AND delete him!*

If you can't bring yourself to do that - go read your reality story from the previous section and ask yourself , 'why the fuck not?'.

If you're struggling to block and delete I want to invite you to ask yourself these questions;

- What are you gaining from NOT blocking and deleting this dickhead?

- Based on the behaviour of the dickhead in question, *what advice would you be giving someone else in this situation?*

- Do you want to be stuck in relationships with dickheads forever?

- What are your concerns about blocking and deleting this dickhead?

- Are these concerns valid enough reasons to not block and delete this dickhead?

Ideally, get a notebook out and explore your answers in writing.

This self-exploration now will save you endless amounts of heartache in the future.

*Make the time to do this work.*

# When you've had children with the dickhead...

The only valid reason I can think that contact would need to remain is if you had children with the dickhead.

In those cases I would personally recommend these actions;

- Still delete and block the dickhead from all other communication except good old fashioned text and phone contact.
- Where possible use a third party to communicate through
- Never reply directly to messages, always type them into the notes on your phone first and wait at least 30 minutes before hitting send
- Where possible have text contact rather than voice calls as texts can be viewed by police if required at any point in cases like harassment. *I would also recommend having a second phone solely to contact the dickhead on so that if your phone is ever required as evidence due to the dickhead being an even bigger dickhead, it's much less of a ball ache for you.*
- KNOWLEDGE IS POWER - do not believe anything the dickhead tells you about your rights as a parent, your legal rights or your financial rights - find out everything for yourself. Dickheads lie.

# #2 - Why you are genuinely better off without them

This is building on the reality story and highlighter exercise.

You're better off without them, you know you are. Nobody needs a dickhead in their life. So, list here, all the reasons that you can think of that you're better off without them;

- 
- 
- 
- 
- 
- 
- 
- 
- 
- 
- 
- 
- 
- 
- 

Fill as many pages as necessary!! Some dickheads need a roll of lining paper to complete this exercise on.

Remember, those sneaky rose-tinted glasses will try and convince you that that list is wrong, and you really do need the dickhead. Make any additional notes you need to here to remind yourself that the rose-tinted spectacles are bollocks and life without the dickhead is better.

Deepening your self-awareness, and
increasing your self-worth will
break the dickhead cycle

A fish who sees the hook for what it is
will never be caught by the fisherman

(What did you actually fall for?)

Over the years one of the questions I've heard women ask the most is this;

*"Why didn't I see it coming?"*

Usually followed up with, *'I should've known better.'*

Let's break this down shall we.

First things first, are you mystic fucking Meg? Do you have a crystal ball?

Are you Doctor Who? Do you have a frigging time machine?

No. No. No.

You're not are you?

Also, on your first date did Mr Dickhead arrive with a neon flashing light on his head that said 'Beware. I'm a dickhead'.

No. He bloody didn't did he?

He turned up looking and sounding and acting like a relatively 'normal' more than likely quite charming human being.

Why would you think anything different????

So, give yourself a break. Know that dickheads actually come in disguise and *quite often put a lot of effort into their disguises!*

But let's explore what it was that you actually fell for initially, because something appealed to you.

Here's a journal prompt to help.

*The things that led me to fall for my latest dickhead were...*

_____

_____

_____

_____

_____

_____

_____

_____

_____

_____

_____

_____

_____

_____

And lets deepen your self-awareness a little further with these journal prompts.

*The feelings and emotions that I was craving from the relationship with my last dickhead were...*

_____

_____

_____

_____

_____

_____

_____

_____

_____

_____

_____

_____

_____

_____

_____

_____

_____

_____

_____

_____

*The experiences I was craving from the relationship with my last dickhead were...*

_____

_____

_____

_____

_____

_____

_____

_____

_____

_____

_____

_____

_____

_____

_____

_____

_____

_____

_____

_____

_____

_____

*I was hoping that my relationship with my latest dickhead would be...*

_____

_____

_____

_____

_____

_____

_____

_____

_____

_____

_____

_____

_____

_____

_____

_____

_____

_____

_____

_____

_____

_____

*What I still crave from a relationship is...*

_____

_____

_____

_____

_____

_____

_____

_____

_____

_____

_____

_____

_____

_____

_____

_____

_____

_____

_____

_____

_____

_____

_____

*These things I crave are important to me because...*

---------------------------------------------------------------

---------------------------------------------------------------

---------------------------------------------------------------

---------------------------------------------------------------

---------------------------------------------------------------

---------------------------------------------------------------

---------------------------------------------------------------

---------------------------------------------------------------

---------------------------------------------------------------

---------------------------------------------------------------

---------------------------------------------------------------

---------------------------------------------------------------

---------------------------------------------------------------

---------------------------------------------------------------

---------------------------------------------------------------

---------------------------------------------------------------

---------------------------------------------------------------

---------------------------------------------------------------

---------------------------------------------------------------

---------------------------------------------------------------

---------------------------------------------------------------

## Time to get that highlighter pen out again.

I want you to re-read your answers to those journal prompts and get lovingly curious - think Jessica Lansbury trying to work out who done it on Murder She Wrote. Curious not self-critical.

I want you to think about what was going on for you; what your own pattern is.

- What are you drawn to?
- What are you craving?
- What is it that keeps you in a cycle of overlooking crappy behaviour and treatment, and allowing yourself to be taken advantage of and disrespected?

You have all the answers within you.

Sometimes it takes a while to see them but the more aware we get of what we're doing and why we're doing it, the easier it is to change things for the better.

Love YOU first

(yep, sounds like a cliché but it's true)

# Love YOU first

I know, I know it sounds like a cliché but it's so true. People who genuinely love and respect themselves don't knowingly stay in relationships with dickheads.

Self-love is nothing to do with being full of yourself, or some sort of diva. It's about having *care and concern for your own wellbeing and happiness, and taking action to secure that happiness.*

Being in a relationship should be an act of self-love not an act of self-harm.

Think about what would be the most loving action that you could take to secure your own present and future happiness, because that's ultimately what's important.

Nobody gets to their deathbed and says 'oh I really regret dumping that absolute wanker who treated me like shit, I wish I'd taken him back and given him another chance.' They do however say things like 'I wish I'd valued my own happiness enough to leave my abusive partner when I had the chance.'

Make decisions from a place of kindness for yourself.

If you have trouble seeing yourself in a positive and deserving light, read on...

## Many many women struggle to love themselves...

Low self-esteem is incredibly common. You might look at other women and think that they all have their shit together and it's only you who's winging in though life, but you'd be very very wrong.

I've sat face to face with many beautiful, talented, intelligent, funny, brilliant women over the years and they have all struggled to like who they are.

Size, race, wealth, privilege etc has nothing to do with it - women struggle.

And it's not hard to see why really. From the moment we pop out of the womb we're inundated with societal messages of how we're meant to look, behave, act, dress etc.

Add that to that things like difficult childhoods with abuse or parental rejection, bullying, workplace bullying, abusive relationships and other issues that affect self-esteem and before you know it you have millions of women all believing they're not good enough, not deserving of happiness and are being 'too much' and 'too demanding' for even daring to suggest they have happy lives.

Well, times they are a changing and women are waking up. Strong feminine energy is rising again like a phoenix and these wounds of old are healing. Women are remembering their worth, remembering their strength and remembering that joy is their birth right. You've awakened by being here, reading this, and I couldn't be happier for you. As Rumi says, 'The wound is the place where the light enters you'. In a weird kind of way we can thank these dickheads for playing a part in the awakening of women.

## How to develop self-love

If you're reading this and thinking 'I'm not sure how to be more self-loving' then don't worry, I'm going to give you some guidance.

Fist of all you need to know this;

## SELF-LOVE IS YOUR NATURAL STATE

You don't actually have to learn anything brand new, *you need to remove what's standing in the way, and to remember the truth.*

When you came into this world you loved who you were. You weren't concerned with trying to be anything other than who you are. You were you and you liked you.

Then somewhere along the lines you started to be told that you weren't clever enough, pretty enough, fast enough, tall enough, thin enough, quiet enough, loud enough, and goodness knows what else and you started to believe these things and question your own value.

**It's time to remember how valuable you are.**

You are enough.

Right here. right now,

you're completely enough.

So, first of all, get clear on how you do see yourself at the moment. It might feel tough and unpleasant to do, but you need to know what you're dealing with in order to change anything.

Describe yourself here, on this page, just scribble down everything that comes to you...

Now, for any negative and unpleasant descriptions of yourself that slipped in there, I want to invite you to get lovingly curious around them;

- Where has that description come from?
- Who told you that thing?
- How true is it? What's the evidence for it?
- Would you call someone else that? If not, why is it OK to call yourself it?
- What are the positive and pleasant things that people say about you? Do you take notice of them?
- How long have I been calling myself these thing?
- Do I want to keep calling myself these things?
- Is there any reason to keep calling myself these things?
- Is there any reason I don't want to stop calling myself these things?

Really explore yourself. Explore what's going on in your thinking and increase your self-awareness.

And know this one thing – YOUR THOUGHTS LIE TO YOU!

Don't believe everything that you think.

Your brain is like a brand new puppy, running about everywhere, peeing everywhere it shouldn't and just doing it's own thing. To behave itself it needs consistent commands. Your brain is the same. It needs you to give it consistent commands. Tell it something long enough and it'll believe it.

When self-esteem is low, *it's because you've heard consistent negative and unpleasant thoughts on repeat so many times that you've accepted them as the truth.*

But they're not true.

Nobody is worthless or useless - that's a bullshit story.

YOU have value.  YOU have worth. You're here on purpose with a purpose - it's time to remember that.

It's time to reconnect to you; to your needs, wants and desires. And it's time to give yourself permission to have them.

It's not easy. When you're in that 'I'm not good enough, and everyone else is better than me' funk. I know, I spent a lot of time there. Here's some suggestions of things to help you;

- Read as many books on self-love as you can.
- Buy self-love affirmation cards to help change your inner dialogue.
- Consistently challenge any unpleasant and unhelpful thoughts.
- Write down all your achievements every day, big or small.
- Push yourself to learn new skills and recognise your own abilities.
- Speak to yourself with kindness (if you wouldn't say it to your best friend, don't say it to yourself.
- Spend time and money on yourself.

- Get support from a coach/therapist/mentor when you need to.

- Check out my website www.lotussoulsister.co.uk

The important thing is to give yourself a place on the priority list - ideally at the top.

♡

I'd like to tell you about a journaling practice I came across a few years ago which helped me to transform my life in so many areas and it works with your self-esteem too.

You basically transport yourself in your imagination to your future self.

To you as the woman who repaired her self-esteem, put herself on the top of the priority list and only allows quality relationships.

And you start to write daily journal entries as if you're already that woman. It's called 'writing your reality'. It really helps to focus your mind on what you want.

I'll show you an example...

At the moment your journal entries might look something like mine did ten years ago...

*'Why me? Why do I always end up with the dickheads? What's wrong with me? Why can't I just find a nice person? I need to lose weight. If I wasn't this fat and ugly they wouldn't treat me this way. I need to be less miserable too. If I was happier, they'd stay. I don't think I'm meant to be happy. Clearly I'm just meant to stay single forever. Maybe I did something in a past life? Maybe I'm being punished. Maybe I should just give up trying.'*

Not a pleasant read but I have a feeling you might recognise elements of that.

Here's how I started to journal instead;

*'Thank God I spent time on myself and making my own happiness a priority because now I love my life! Now I feel confident, clear, focused and strong. I know what I want and what I don't want. I know my own mind. I control the quality of what I allow into my thoughts. I support myself, I cheer myself on, I allow myself to be happy. I only have room in my life for valuable relationships. I spot a dickhead a mile off and they get no place in my life - I value my peace and happiness. I feel calm daily, I feel happy daily, I feel proud of myself daily. I help other women steer clear of dickheads and find quality relationships.'*

Do you see the difference? Do you feel the different energy?

When I first started writing like this every day, I was nowhere near that second entry, but bit by bit, decision by decision and day by day I got exactly there. *I highly recommend doing this journal practice as often as you can.*

# The real truth about the 'dickhead magnet'

(This might sting a bit - sorry about that)

There is no dickhead magnet,

You don't actually attract them.

Dickheads gravitate towards everyone.

But here's the truth and it's possibly an even more uncomfortable truth in some ways that possessing a dickhead magnet.

*You allow the dickhead to stay.*

That's the difference.

You allow them to stay. You give them permission to be in your life. You give them permission to ruin and take over your life.

Ouch.

Told you it was a little uncomfortable.

And now you're probably thinking 'WTAF? Why do I do that? What's wrong with me??'. Well, it's usually one of these things (or a combination of them)...

- *You've never been shown what a healthy relationship looks like so you genuinely don't know any better*

- *Your self-esteem needs work*

- *You've been gaslighted/mentally abused*

So let's look at those 3 in a bit more detail...

Can you recognise a healthy relationship?

(Lots of people have never seen one)

We can often spend so much time beating ourselves up for the fact that we've got involved with yet another dickhead, and miss the fact that maybe we don't actually know what a non-dickhead really 'looks' like.

Think about the relationships you've witnessed - your parents, your grandparents, your friends relationships, your siblings relationships.

How healthy are they?

Often, clients have come to me in the past bereft following the fall-out of yet another catastrophic relationship with a dickhead, but when we explore the relationships they've grown up around, they were bloody awful relationships too.

So ponder on that for a moment - *what have you been shown by the relationships you've grown up around?*

Arguing? - Violence? - cheating? - lying? - never apologising? - the silent treatment? - blame? - zero constructive conversations? - control?

What have you witnessed and therefore internalised?

Have you been shown kindness, genuine affection with no conditions attached to it, support. forgiveness, constructive conversations?

*We usually copy what we know.* Use the journal prompt on the next page to explore this.

What I've witnessed and realised from the relationships I've grown up around is...

_____
_____
_____
_____
_____
_____
_____
_____
_____
_____
_____
_____
_____
_____
_____
_____
_____
_____
_____
_____
_____
_____
_____
_____

I can use this awareness to positively impact my future relationships by...

_____

_____

_____

_____

_____

_____

_____

_____

_____

_____

_____

_____

_____

_____

_____

_____

_____

_____

_____

_____

_____

_____

Are you allowing yourself to be fed the crumbs because you don't feel like you deserve the whole cake?

(Where is your self-esteem at?)

# Low self-esteem

In very simple terms, your self-esteem is how valuable or worthy you feel you are. It's kind of like, if you were for sale in a shop - what price tag would you put on yourself? Often, when self-esteem is low, there is no price - the person feels like they're worth nothing. And when you feel like you're worth nothing, you give yourself away for free all the time.

Deep down though, your soul screams at you in the voice of unpleasant emotion, because it knows the truth - that you are completely and utterly priceless. And that's why it feels so terrible to have low self-esteem. It's not your natural state - it's not how things are meant to be and your emotions tell you that.

*Improving your self-esteem is really the most effective weapon in the fight against getting stuck in relationships with dickheads.*

When self-esteem increases these things take care of themselves;

Boundaries, assertiveness, confidence, self-worth.

It's like something clicks inside you and you just can't allow yourself to be stuck with a dickhead - it becomes excruciatingly painful and if one has happened to slip under your dickhead radar, you get rid of them quick.

In fact, you stop settling in all areas of life.

If you feel your self-esteem is low, know that it absolutely can be fixed.
*(See the additional resources at the end of this guide for more help)*

# Mental abuse - Gaslighting - Narcissism

In addition to rebuilding your self-esteem, one of the best gifts you'll ever give yourself is to educate yourself around these subjects. I'll give you the skeleton here, but please, please, please look into this further if this is a new subject to you.

It's been a factor in almost every dickhead story I've heard over the last 10 years, including my own.

Mental abuse is usually recognised as having occurred by these symptoms - chronic anxiety, depression and PTSD.

Mental abuse basically affects the way you think - it distorts your thinking. Think of it a bit like having a virus in your computer - it fucks up the programming and it stops working as it's meant to.

In terms of dating dickheads, it's very possible that they have created the initial mental abuse, and then once the relationship is over, and they're not in contact with you any more, you keep that abuse fresh by continuing with self-hatred. This is why self-love and restoring your self-esteem is so incredibly crucial and ideally wants to become your number 1 priority if you feel like you've been a victim of mental abuse.

It can be repaired, but it's like having a broken leg and staying at home instead of going to the hospital. Unless you're an expert in fixing broken legs - get help fixing it. Same with self-esteem and recovering from mental abuse - get help with it. It's easier, quicker and much less painful.

# Gaslighting

'Gaslighting' became a term to describe a particular type of psychological abuse following the creation of the film 'Gas light' in 1938. Google it and watch a bit, it's incredibly powerful.

Basically, it's a manipulation technique to gain power over someone and to make them question their own sanity.

It's bloody awful, and the thing about it, that makes it so awful, is that the way it's done is so bloody sneaky, that you can be well into a relationship, and incredibly brainwashed effectively, before you even suspect anything is wrong. It's incredibly destructive and it's possibly one of the strongest things I've seen that keeps people tied to incredibly toxic relationships. Even above fear, the effects of gaslighting keep people very stuck indeed.

A gas lighter will leave you feeling mentally weak, reliant on them to make decisions, confused, incredibly confused - you will think at times that you're going mad.

One of the main signs that show you might well have a gas lighter around you is that you feel a strong need to record your conversations with them. If you're in a relationship now and you're having to do that for your own sanity;

- GET THE FUCK OUT!!!!!

A gas lighter will recall different memories of events, they will tell you you've done something when you haven't and visa versa.

They will call you 'mad', 'mental', say you 'need help' and that you're 'not normal'.

They will question your sanity so many times that you won't know which way is up any more.

Do not waste your time wondering if the gas lighter is aware they are doing this or not. Get out of the relationship if you've identified this is happening, and work on repairing your mind before you even try to repair the relationship (if that's something you even want to do).

Staying with a gas lighter will only make you second guess yourself constantly, feel confused all the time, become increasingly anxious, and destroy your self-esteem because you'll always be feeling like there's something wrong with you.

Gaslighting doesn't just occur in romantic relationships, so be aware. It could be a parent, sibling, child, boss - anyone. Educate yourself on this subject as much as you possibly can.

A simple Google search will give you loads of good information as a starting point.

# Narcissism

Narcissism is where someone is completely self-absorbed, and it's often what people worry they'll turn into if they start to prioritise their own needs and desires.

There's a big difference between someone who just really likes themselves and is potentially quite vain, and someone who is a narcissist, so be careful with this one.

Often, I've found that when clients are calling their ex a narcissist, they weren't - they were actually someone who was being mentally and emotionally abusive and gas lighting.

The problem with a narcissist is that *they will always always care about themselves more than they care about you* - you will always come second - always.

They will want to be the 'leader' of everything, so that means they'll want to lead you, and for you to basically do what you're told - they like to control.

They are arrogant and feel entitled all the time.

This personality is hard work to be around, because everything has to be their way, on their terms, to their liking, and quite simply, they don't give a shit what you think. This is their 'nature', 'personality' - whatever you want to call it. You won't change it, so don't bother trying. Ask yourself this question 'is it worth putting up with this for the rest of my life?'

Because that's how long they'll be a narcissist for.

Beware the vulnerable narcissist. This type is the even more sneaky sucker and potentially the type that the majority of people who've felt like they've attracted dickheads has encountered.

These ones pull on the heart strings of the nice person.

This type of personality feels very inadequate beneath their surface - you can probably spot that a mile off, which is why you tolerate it. It's the 'awwwww but they're a good person underneath' button.

These people are incredibly sensitive, fear being abandoned, often suicidal, and have terrible self-esteem themselves. However, the thing to be very mindful of with any type of narcissist (and I strongly urge you to research them) is that they have a distinct lack of empathy. They do not give a shit. They will bleed you dry. They will take your time, your money, your energy - anything that suits them and works to their advantage to get their needs met - and they will never return the favour. Knowingly staying with a narcissist is accepting that the relationship will always be one sided and always on their terms. If you're OK with that, go for it. The choice is always yours.

But remember this truth - *you will NOT change a narcissist.*

Your energy is too precious to waste trying
to work them out

(Be thankful that your brain isn't wired up in the same
way)

Wanting to understand them and work out 'why' can drive you round the bend.

Is there really a decent reason to do this to yourself?

I know we have a desire to work things out in our heads - to make sense of things and to understand other people but sometimes the only truth to be found is 'they're just a dickhead'.

Energy can only focus on one thing at a time, so ask yourself '*what do I want to spend my precious energy on?*'.

Working them out, or working on yourself so that this dickhead cycle ends.

Because the thing is, you'll never understand fully. You're chasing something more rare than rocking horse shit. *They* don't even know why they're a dickhead, and if you think you can somehow magically get them to understand themselves, change and apologise, then please have a little word with yourself, because that is NOT going to happen.

Look at your own life. Look at how difficult it is to work yourself out, know why you've ended up with dickheads, change yourself and improve yourself. It's hard, right? So if it's that hard to change yourself, how hard is it to change someone else? Bloody impossible! *Save your strength, and focus on YOU!*

Every day is a school day

(Every dickhead teaches you something)

I remember sitting down at the laptop in 2015 and opening 4 Word documents. Each one had the name of a dickhead I'd dated that year. Sadly this wasn't my entire quota of dickheads - there has been more.

But 2015 had been a particularly dickhead-full year.

I started to type away at the laptop about each relationship, with the aim being to focus on what had i learned.

I decided to take a deep breath and explore these relationships from every angle I could think of;

- What had I learned about myself?
- What red flags were there that I'd missed?
- What would I go back and tell myself in that relationship?
- What had I realised about them?
- What would I never do again?
- What had gone well?
- Why was I drawn to that relationship?
- What kept me in that relationship after I knew it was no good for me?
- What did my intuition sound and feel like in that relationship?
- What wisdom would I pass on from being in that relationship?
- What advice would I give to the next woman who gets in a relationship with that dickhead?

These were some of the best pieces of writing I've ever done and I definitely encourage you to do the same.

*Exploration like this prepares the ground for your future happiness.*

This pause, this reflection and this attention on learning stops the automatic flow of dickhead to dickhead.

*It interrupts the cycle.*

And that's what you want - *awareness.*

It stops you blindly going on an autopilot mission into another shitter of a relationship.

So, if you want happier relationships in the future;

DO THE WORK!


Expecting things to change without putting in any effort
is like waiting for a ship at the airport.

Are you secretly choosing dickheads

(Don't instantly dismiss this - you might be)

Of course we'd love to think that we always try and choose the best possible partners for ourselves, but lets explore this a little.

Most of us don't operate from a place of being wide awake and self-loving. Lots and lots of us, are operating from a place of subconscious auto-pilot based on low self-esteem. This can lead us to make some seriously crap choices.

So, before we go any further, grab a pen and write an answer to this journal prompt;

I secretly *choose* dickheads because...

_____

_____

_____

_____

_____

_____

_____

_____

_____

_____

_____

_____

_____

_____

Did you find anything tucked away in your subconscious there? It's amazing what a journal prompt can uncover.

Remember to never judge or get self-critical over your answers. Exploring yourself in this way is brave - very brave. Most people never get this far.

Always congratulate yourself for the things that you discover - even if they do at times sting like a bitch. *This awareness will make you a happier, wiser, stronger person from this moment onwards.*

So, here's some reasons I've come across over the years as to why we secretly choose dickheads. Some are mine, some are from my clients. See if you can identify with any of these;

- You feel uncomfortable with 'nice' partners. Dickheads are familiar, so you stay with the 'devil you know'.
- You like to play the martyr.
- You like to be the one who's always seen as the saint in the relationship - you look less dickhead-ish when you're with a bigger dickhead.
- You don't feel like you deserve anything better (low self-esteem).
- Unresolved emotional distress/trauma.
- You genuinely don't know what love, particularly unconditional love looks like.
- Fear. Plus potential fear of commitment - you know deep down that a relationship with a dickhead isn't likely to last long-term.
- You're familiar with emotional pain, so you gravitate towards and stay in familiar relationships.

# Moving Forward

(Decide now what your future will look like)

Find your own closure.


(Because they ain't gonna give you it)

I'm telling you this with love, even though it sounds blunt. Because here's the thing - you could wait your entire lifetime for 'closure' in the form of an apology or a reason or something.

It's important to know what you're actually wanting if you're craving 'closure'. What is it that you need? And get real with yourself, is it going to happen in the way that you want?

If a person has been an absolute twat for weeks, months, years, decades - however long you've known them - are they seriously going to just change and start considering your feelings and telling you the truth?

No. No they're not.

So, instead of throwing all the power their way all the time and needing their answers, and their reasons, and to know the workings of their mind - *take your power back and find your own closure.*

Write the end of the chapter how you need to write it.

Create your own story - your own closure.

And I seriously hope it goes something along the lines of;

*"and she learned the lessons she needed to learn, she broke the cycle once and for all, moved on with her life and never settled for another dickhead again."*

# Create your future

(Set your new standards)

OK, time to get clear on what the future is going to look like.

For those of you into manifesting, this is where you set your clear intentions as to what you want.

Let's get really really clear on what you're going to accept in future relationships and what you're not.

Things to consider;

- Set the standards for your initial dates. Will a coffee at Costa cut it or do you want to be wined and dined?
- Set the standards for how you expect to be spoken to.
- Decide what are non-negotiables in your relationship
- Set the boundaries for sex - how soon is too soon?
- Set the boundaries for living together

Write out what a typical day in the life of your perfect relationship would be like. Would you be brought a cup of tea in bed, or maybe you're an early bird and would be the one to put.the kettle on. Would your ideal partner work, or maybe you'd prefer someone retired or who works from home. Would you enjoy the same things? What would you talk about? How would you feel throughout the day? Would you text each other during the day or would you catch up over a dinner out most evenings?

There are no rights or wrongs to this, and of course it's always going to change as you grow and evolve and your interests change, but many people have never even sat down to consider what they really and truly want, so if that's you, now is your chance to get some clarity and focus.

My new relationship standards are...

_____

_____

_____

_____

_____

_____

_____

_____

_____

_____

_____

_____

_____

_____

_____

_____

_____

_____

An ex is an ex for a reason

(Don't forget the bloody reasons!!)

Again, drum it into your mindset now. What are the reasons that your ex, or exes are exes?

Also known as, *what will I not put up with again?*

Get them written down;

- 
- 
- 
- 
- 
- 
- 
- 
- 
- 
- 
- 
- 

**An ex is an ex for a reason!!**

# Your dickhead radar

You've explored a lot in this guide. And this is YOUR dickhead repellent manual, so what are your top takeaways? *What will be the red flags on your dickhead radar?*

What are the things you vow to never forget so that you can move towards a life of more happiness and more fulfilling relationships?

Everyone can be a bit of a dickhead


(Just decide on your own level of dickhead)

## An important note to remember...

Here's the thing. Everyone has a bit of dickhead in them. I can be a dickhead, you can be a dickhead, I'm sure even saints have the occasional moment of dickhead. That's humans being human. And in relationships it's important to remember that.

You're not perfect 100% of the time and your partner isn't going to be either. Accept that.

Relationships also take work. Accept that and accept your part in that.

It's not your job to make your partner happy, and it's not their job to make you happy.

But it is both of your jobs to make sure you're not intentionally making the other one unhappy.

Make communication a priority. Never expect someone else to be a mind reader. If you have a problem - tell them. If you've been a dickhead, apologise. If they've been a dickhead, tell them and give them the opportunity to apologise. Sometimes we're dickheads by accident.

Know your non-negotiables and communicate them.

Choose wisely and keep constantly evaluating your own happiness.

# You legend!

If you made it to this part of this guide, you're an absolute legend and I have so much faith and confidence that your dickhead days are over.

But, don't get complacent!

Stay open to see the good in everyone you meet, be hopeful that they'll be wonderful, and treat them as if they are - but be on your guard - listen to your dickhead radar, and when it starts sending you red flags, drop that slimy sucker like a hot potato!

On the next two pages are some affirmations to keep your mindset on the right tracks, and also a couple of pages for notes.

You're awesome, you deserve the best, now go forth and ditch dickheads forever.

Sending you lots of love on your zero dickhead journey,

*Wendy xx*

# Affirmations

I'm only available for quality relationships now

I do not date dickheads

I'm worthy of quality relationships

Wonderful relationships exist and I deserve one

My relationship with myself sets the standard for all other relationships

I love myself first

I respect myself

I am committed to my own health and happiness

I do not tolerate disrespectful behaviour towards me

It's safe for me to be without a partner

# Affirmations

A partner is an added bonus to my already wonderful life

Quality relationships bring value to my life, not misery

You do not find a happy life - you make it

My happiness is my responsibility

I respect myself and my happiness enough to maintain my boundaries

I'm committed to only allowing quality relationships into my life

♡

# MY NOTES

# MY NOTES

## About the author
## - Wendy Middlehurst -

I'm not going to do that weird thing where you write in the third person as if some fancy team wrote your copy.

I have no team lol. I do all this stuff myself. Unless you class my needy border collie, Winston, as a team member. He certainly likes to make an appearance on my Facebook lives.

So, what shall I tell you about me? This is why other people get a team to write them! It's so weird.

Well, I've dated a lot of dickheads, I think you gathered that one. I swear a lot. You probably noticed that one too. I'm from the North East of the UK. I'm a trained bereavement and therapeutic counsellor, an energy healer, an angel guide and I help women improve their self-esteem and evolve into the best possible version of themselves.

I'm a mum of 3 children, all growing up way too fast. I love to be on the beach. I love to drink cocktails (preferably on a nice beach) and thankfully after numerous disaster relationships I finally found a non dickhead (well, he's a tiny bit of a dickhead, but he's my dickhead - and I genuinely bought him a keyring with that on - which he used) on a dating app of all places.

So, keep the faith! - you never know who your next date will bring you - it might just be the dickhead you always wanted.

# More helpful resources from the author

*'Step Away From The Dickhead!'* -
A Free Facebook group to get support completing this book and also connect with other women who get what it's like to be stuck in the dickhead cycle.

*'The Gateway'* -
A private Facebook community to continue your personal-development and self-love journey where my *'Beginning to love yourself'* course is held.

*'Beginning to love yourself'* - self-help guide & journal
*'Affirmations for the soul'* - affirmation cards
*'Affirmations for the soul'* - book
*'Release your grief'* - book - my personal account of how I found healing following the death of my absent father.

1-2-1 Private counselling sessions

(Details can also be found at www.lotussoulsister.co.uk)

My books are also available on Amazon  - search my name;
*Wendy Middlehurst.*

Lotus Soul Sister

@wendymiddlehurst_author

Printed in Great Britain
by Amazon